POETIC DIARY

WRITTEN BY:

TRACEY RENEE HOWARD

ISBN: 1-4107-5765-X (e-book)
ISBN: 1-4107-5764-1 (Paperback)

This book is printed on acid free paper.

1stBooks – rev. 09/18/03

This Book Is **Dedicated** To My:

Mom: Mable Howard, the one who shared with me life, love and independence. **Sisters**: Maxine Howard, she has been one of my close friends throughout my entire life, we hit it off the first day I came home from the hospital and we had to share the same crib and Sharon Vann for her spiritual guidance and unconditional big sister love and support. **Brother**: Felix Howard for being there when I needed him the most and ALL of my **Nieces** and **Nephews** for sharing their unconditional love that brings me indescribable joy.

POETIC CONTENTS

ACKNOWLEDGEMENTS

No matter how independently strong you are, the fact remains people need people. Without the love and support of family and friends this would have not materialized, thank you all.

I would also like to give a personal shout out to my girl Tonya for her consistent sincere encouragement and support through good and not so good times.

Photograph by Danielle Weldon.

FAMILY CUSHION

MABLE

My mama, gave me birth to life
cocked open her legs
and pushed out her baby girl into this world
though I was not suppose to exist
when she saw me she couldn't resist

Sweat, tears, heartache
was apart of our experience
yet cause Mable is who she is
it fostered nothing but brilliance
while holding on to resilience
for life preparations diligence

"Now baby girl
I don't have far in school's education
yet this common sense iza hear teaching you
will help you supersede the best of any president
though they may want you to kiss some butt
never surrender to it's emptiness
cause your worth is way far too much"

Okay Ma,
I respect what you say, yet you know
I'm gonna do my thang, my way

Yet in appreciation of you being you
THANKS
for melting the king of dark chocolates
and allowing him
to crack your precious eggs
making your heart sang melodies of
freedom, peace, justice and truth
I'm proud to have come from
the wisdom of your cocked open legs

Love you Ma!

MY DADDY

My Daddy loved me for me
I was his baby girl – little Percell

When I cried & fussed to go back with my Mommy
he would just shake his head and say girl you are a mess
but nevertheless granted my request

My daddy made it known to the world I was his treasure
and as long as he lived he would disown me never

I know for a fact I worked his nerves
but never once did he make me feel his love was undeserved

I was six years old when my daddy died
and oh boy did I cry, tears still fall from my eyes
making melodies with my cries

No matter how much I mature
my heart will continue to yearn for nature
and that is to have my daddy's active love
a blessing I've been shortchanged of

My daddy had a strong personality along with a big heart
I have definitely inherited my part
He was also honest coupled with bold
which too is a part of my fold

He would understand my strong stance
and would laugh at anyone
who was afraid to ask me to dance

Oh yes he would say you are definitely mine
look there are my genes running down your line
Baby girl never be ashamed of who you are
it's their fault if they can't see a shining star

Thank you for loving me for me
I miss you Daddy!

BEST FRIEND

Someone who allows you to love them without any fear
who tells you the truth
even if it doesn't bring you good cheer
one who is not jealous of your talents
consistently there to help despite
you feeling it's too much of a challenge

Someone who does not judge you for being you
even when knowing your deep inner faults
they don't make you feel they're better off

Someone who never lets you down
despite at times, you acting like a clown
One you can trust with your life
even when it means the ultimate personal sacrifice

Who will be that someone to carry out all the above
The one and only True God
who master the quality Love

JUSTIN

He's innocent and trusting
this baby boy fills my heart with joy
cute as can be one can see
and I'm not saying this
cause he's related to me

Notice his eyes when he smiles
can't you see the stars
floating from his profile

He goes by the name of Justin
and please don't underestimate him
he's truly something

Just because he's only two
take it from his auntie who
knows him through and through
His capabilities of melting your heart
is definitely on of his arts

Auntie Loves you forever Justin!

MASCULINE MAN

I've met a man not long ago
who truly is a masculine man
he's spiritual, sensitive, smart and sweet
meeting him was truly a treat

My feeling was not always this way
he said some things that dampened my day
he told me I was in transition
I felt his comment to be somewhat offensive

Who was this man to read my circumstance
especially since he was never around to see me dance
he spoke to me with confidence and familiarity
which made me challenge his formality

Well time went on and proved at this time he was right
I was in the middle of strife
when looking back I no longer resent
the counsel this masculine man sent

I've learned many things from this man
which will enable me to further my plan
respect for headship is divine
which was hard for me to see
through these imperfect eyes

But when the door was opened
and I was allowed to look inside
I finally understood the going on of men minds

For this lesson I'm forever grateful
it has aided in helping me keep my way successful

BABY KIRAH

Baby Kirah is kind, sensitive, spiritual,
sweet, and thoughtful
her qualities are her rituals

She has grown up and is now a young lady
unbelievable to me possessing the
capabilities of having her own babies

When did all this time pass bye
it's making me want to cry

Nonetheless I'm happy and proud
that she's my niece
My Baby Kirah
showers me with inner peace

BLOCK PARTY

The block party on the bus was tight
we had us a good ole ruckus
playing music laughing bout good times
recognizing life is short
seeing the value of its escort

Drinking, sipping, dipping in and out
with love floating shouts of dove's connection
to Nat and Peaches
which puts us in the mind of the movie Beaches

Best friends forever through thick and thin
though one is gone
she keeps shining with a grin
solid as gold, never turning old, just wiser
accepting all underneath her wing
mixing melodies of rap and jazz
until it sings sweet rings of music healing tone
bringing cushion to a core of stone

We can't forget about Milton, cause without him
the Hilton wouldn't exist
with its embassy suites
making everything run smoothly and sweet

it's where the rock got his foundation
embracing all the coalitions with limitless hesitation
and though the boat rocks back and forth
it never tips over
while quivering in its spot
all along holding down life's shock

Streaming forward we all go knowing
time will help us heal as we absorb enemy's steel
robbing us of precious stones and diamonds
buried underground in earth's dirt
we heard no sound for that instant
all in a trance
in disbelief of our now distance

Came to embracing Shanise dance
always she prance with dignity's grace
still holding on to this rat race
who stole her brother/best friend in the night
elegantly standing tall
not losing sight of being alive
appreciating their siblings as anchors on each side

We Stand, We Fall, We Stand, We Fall
Again and Again and Again

Getting back on the bus that's packed with fun
of good ole times that none of us
would transfer for a Trillion Dimes
simply cause it can't be bought
we gotta appreciate times bank
never relinquishing our vulnerability to sank

We accept the invitation to the block party
that made our hearts
Sang with Laughter
Cry for Healing
Dance with Joy
in history trance we acknowledge
Mr. Nat Grand
never ever dismissing our Father's Gift of Life

So remember no matter where we've
been, gone, seen or done
we all must let life's circle bring us back
to the block party on the bus
and enjoy the Shower of its Sun

Dedicated to Peaches... Love You!

MY BROTHA

You are it
simply cause you take much stuff
even when you had enough
of life's disappointment
you press on in the midst of scorn
making me see the value of why you were born

Teaching silently through guilt falls
accepting gifts delicacies without spoil
adding sweet funk aroma to flava
not giving favors to the value of self taught
is where you've been purchased and bought

Though you fight grace truth
not ready to call it truce on the battle
simply accepting the will for others to follow
life's reality rejecting possible fatalities
while biting the bullet with a vest
you've taught me power's invest

SHARINE

Listen to the name it truly has a nice ring
a ring that no song could out sing
this ring is unique made up of melodies
only Sharine could sing

These melodies are made up
of Sharine's personality
which brought her in touch with life's realities
these realities sometimes brought her gloom
but as we know Sharine nothing could stop her
from sharing that fabulous smile
when walking into a room

Sharine was known for her determination
willing to pay the cost despite discrimination
zeal for true worship was evident
her time in sacred service took precedence

Sharine strived for faithfulness to the end
remaining our Father's loyal friend
may we imitate this aspect of her life
and never get tired of fighting the fight

Remember to keep your ears open for that ring
this is how we will identify Sharine

When the resurrection finally take place
let's watch for her fabulous smile
which will brighten Bessie's face

THE WOMB

The womb we've shared
magnetic energy delivered us here

Our bond will be a lifetime
it's intricate design is sublime

Juices we've inherited coast through veins
dictating our behavior never be estranged

Difficult it is since we live different lives
one obviously not wisely chosen
but nonetheless still golden

The womb we shared did not spare its gifts
If we open our eyes we'll see it's right in our midst

So lets take hold like when we first came out
and allow our entire souls to joyfully shout

SISTAH, SISTAH!

My sweet dear Sistah
whom I love very much
there is no one in the world
that can replace her special touch
she has been by my side all of my life
her love is evident in my eye sight

My Sistah is beautiful in and out
that's a fact without a doubt
ever since my Sistah was a little girl
she never allowed anyone to bother my curls
and they better not call her little sister fat
she was the only one who could do that

We grew up and became teenagers
hanging out with all kinds of strangers
we both thought we were grown
going out dancing late at night
causing our mother to moan

Believe it or not Sistah is now a mother too
understanding what we put our mother through
It is truly amusing to hear her rant and rave
she sounds as if she totally forgot about the old days

But then again maybe that's why she carries on so
wanting to protect her baby girl from life's woes
Oh yeah, my Sistah will protect her own
even if her kids have to become
prisoners in their own home

And no one better not interfere
if they don't want to shed any tears
don't get me wrong, I think it's all good
we would be better off if we had more Sistahs
like Maxine in the neighborhood

I love you forever my Sistah, Sistah!

LIVING LIFE'S CIRCLE

SPRING

Spring makes you want to sing
enjoying it's melodious ring
It makes you want to fall in love
and glide through a pond like a dove

Spring makes you want to walk for miles
wearing a great big smile
It helps you appreciate children's laughter
listen to them giggle
watching their little bodies wiggle
running with sparkles in their eyes
cute as can be we can't deny

Spring has a way of introducing you to life
and when analyzed is full of spice
spice when is used adds zest
having the tendency to bring out the best

Spring can have many affects
makes you feel close to perfect
so let's just kick back in our hearts and sing
enjoying every day of this spring

HIP HOP

Hip Hop sticks to my ribs
it's the foundation of many cribs
being evolved in the heart of South Bronx
where many experienced hard knocks

Rejection from corporate authority
turned it's backs on talent
insinuating their check books
couldn't be balanced

Halfhearted opportunities were extended
as long as one was willing to stay in the kitchen
now tell me how was a man suppose to swallow that
it was an impossible request that deserved a smack

And so to the streets and parks they went
competing with one another for best raps on end
break dancing and rapping was their way in finding solace
while caressing the turntables minds went soaring

Addida sneakers and bamboo earrings
slapped five with the streets
daring anyone to challenge it's funky beats

Let's just see how we gonna make it big
despite at this time not owning a twig

All the crews had Hip Hops back
the Casanova's made sure of that
with the support of it's own
they were sure to turn gold

10 years later there goal turned platinum
leaving greedy hands
wanting a piece of the action

Oh how quickly the tables has turned
even their little girls
want a piece of Hip Hop's man

An amazing empire they built with their own hands
which is why we must grace them
with a standing ovation
for their determination
despite discrimination

So no matter what people say
you go head and get yours anyway
make your dream come true
the way Hip Hop demonstrated for you

SWEET DREAMS

Convincing the convinced is not in my defense case

while the team dreams, you'll detect my scheme is clean

calculating value's cent of justice books crooked cell

begging to be released from hell of judgment punishment

falling I stand tall through it all

in appreciation for life's freedom gift

I accept sweet dreams of life mercy

RACISM

Who you blaming for your gray skies, racism
I don't think so
has anyone told you it's time to let go
of this non-existing woe
devalued price tag world's public hoe

Who you mad at for your circumstances
as you claim racism stipulation on freedom's dance
while ignoring multiplied opportunities
for instruction rules game
the nucleus talent reacts on subliminal delusions
confused crying to reject excuses

Racism existence was created for capitalisms success
It's all about the Benjamin's Baby
yep it was your brother that was shady
he made the trade for your grave

Open your eyes and accept the truth
calling it truce on racism
while letting capitalism confirm
your dignity with its green

MY PENNY

If the tag says 99 cents
why do you keep my dolla
give me my penny
cause if not you will hear me holla

It's only a penny you say
then why are you trying to keep it
don't even try to underestimate the wit
100 pennies amounts to a dolla
and that's been taught
by all household Mama's

Is it your checking account you only want fat
dismissing my potential to increase my stats
let me share with you one valuable fact
monetary gain is for all who's willing to reach
so how bout you respect the contract and not breach

So reach in that register and give my penny
before I holla
cause 100 pennies amounts to a dolla

SUMMER

Summer blooms activities of fresh sweet sweat
streaming down the face, rolling on the neck
captivating the absorption of sun rays
as it swirls desirable on golden skin
enticing the bodies to have fun with sin

Flirting, smiling, feeling array
rejoicing over the dismissal of winter dismay
lime, orange, peach and white
are summer breeze color bright delights
chocolate, vanilla, strawberry and cream
enjoying water sprinkles tickling screams

Running from the coach baseball team
and it's desire to hit a home run
despite the humidity blazing sun
it's summer's fun vacation day
let's make sure we enjoy its short stay

PARADISE GARAGE

The paradise garage was the place to be
when you needed to be set free
from life's stipulation and discrimination
do to the lack of human civilities in many communities

Wanting to help folks melt off stress
Larry Lavon got dressed and impressed
many of its subjects through house music funky beats
that are still reminiscence on new york city streets

Hundreds upon hundreds had its membership
feeding the craving for its authenticity
racing to be drowned out by its god like speakers
causing folks to bow down surrendering sneakers

As it's rhythms violently caressed ears
bringing so many to tears
as zig zag beats were felt everywhere

Dancing for nights on end
as vibrations rocked the universe
trembling souls in its skin insinuating deliberate sins
for instant gratifications of the ultimate high
despite years later for actions sighs

Heads rocked to the beat until out of control
causing eyes to roll through ones head
signifying pupils were being fed
by the pulse of tweeters explosions
not being aware of its upcoming erosions

Being programmed into a trance
by a song you couldn't stand
was his technique that was unique
which kept everyone on their feet
until your soul felt it was wrapped up deep
in it's fleece experiencing peace

All walks of life was its background
black, latino, white, straight, gay, rich, poor, male,
female, young, old, hip, square…the garage didn't care

It welcomed you because you were you
as long as you lavished in its beats
while enjoying the intensity of its heat

Though some wanted it shut down
signals were given when the frowns were around
color green meant they were seen
red led to the door and
white in seeking to disrupt skins

The crowd was so punching tight
even when searching
there was nothing in sight to find
for goodness sake you could barely move
but amazingly somehow everyone still felt their groove
at house music capitol

That place will be remembered forever
simply because it was the singular escape
that brought many folks pleasure
I tell you if you heard him once
you would have been convinced
Larry Lovan was the premium DJ
of paradise garage, house funk

LIFE'S CONFUSION

Life's confusion can sometimes be amusing
when your situation is not limited
to stipulations justice money
inability to be bring in the honey
for your pride to maintain its stride

It has the insolence to run and hide
without leaving a guide
to help you fight away heavy water tides
that's rising up to your thighs

Even when you know the grand plan
your only role in playing in the band
is to tell and stand yet the water still rise
high pass the thighs, creeping to the neck
making you scream what the heck

Because you can't seem to find
your deck of faith that's been misplaced
so you clasp your hands, bow your head
and began to cry knowing
without this you will surely die

Life's confusion has claimed your faith has gone under
just when you thought it was all you had left
it's been announced, there has been a grand theft

Mmmmh......life is full of confusion
and we must continue to laugh at its delusion
until sweet truth brings it all to its conclusion

We must have laughter to prevent going insane
cause baby that's truly the name of the game
to keep one senses through it all
when it appears the only outcome is to fall
maintain your core in life's confusion!

SOFT WORDS

Soft words when painted
gives greenness and laughter
to eye shadows
teaching the will of love

DIGNITY'S RAPE

74 billion dollars is what you want
for the comfort of your ego
ya never dreamed the man ruling
the world would be so despicable
killing, slaying, raping, molesting
the human family not giving any empathy
to the power of love chastity

Bombing, beating, stripping
a nation of right's dignity for greed power
look at yourself in the mirror
can't you see your soul is sour
wanting to add Hope in misery's mire

Okay how bout we do it the
Justice for all way
put your soul where your mouth is
let your family be in front of war lines
if you claiming to be sublime
add Congress' in their too
since their supporting these efforts through and through

And if you're still standing when it's all done
and can reminisce about the fun
turning your face to the sun
giving grace for peace on earth
then surely it proves your actions
are a disgrace to the human race

I have to admit, can't be all that mad
cause it's fulfilling the bigger and better grand plan
and though I may express thoughts of the mind
it's all neutrality in this here heart
believe me I don't want no parts
this here poem is just a part of the
ARTS

COLOR NUTRIENTS

Tree's Brown roots sleep

Yellow sun green leaves

fun life's laughter

Blue ocean water

exfoliate souls escape

Accept color's nutrients

BLACK BALLING

Are you aware of the conspiracy on our men
and system prevention for them to stand
enjoying dance
for ego's health to bring wealth's smile
to family peace

As the shadow lingers ahead sweating and
beseeching its game on the mind
that they don't think we recognize
as they hide behind its veil
that has caused many private cells hell

Due to its insecurity guilt and fear
who degradingly forced hundred of millions
to pay severe for their dark amber brilliance
who they've locked away in prison
proving the fact of black balling existence

Sensitivity and ignorance is what they blame
for ones not getting grip on America's fame

Reality has different out comes for those on the
Board of Directors
ya know there's only one on Board

and you best believe he ain't
in charge of calculating scores
though his intelligence supersedes qualifications
suggestions are ignored
when sharing communications

Frustrating it is rightfully so
but we all must continue to grip the ride
and ladies if you hear me
we all need to stand by our brother's side

And yes we're dealing with many issues
keeping it real, means knowing the deal
so aim your arrows where it should be
at conspiracy wheel
cause that's what's making us all ill

As women we are carrying our own
but to close our eyes to our brother's plight
will not erase the pain in our heart's sight

Ya see, sooner or later we gonna have to deal
cause when our son is born
they too will see him as enemies thorn
even if his blood percent
is the grain size of the corn

So how bout if we acknowledge the facts
and always give our brothers a pat on the back
for their involuntarily endurance
of ignorance heat
it is the weak who
agreed for our men to be black balled

It's justifiable if you're appalled
raise your head erect and tall
letting it be felt we ain't giving
up until the situation melts
And that's simply because we care
and want justice served everywhere

Dedicated to the Brothas!

SUMMER MOON

Summer moon speaks to you at night

as it grace you with its sight

stars rain reflections on silk waters

whispering in your ears

bringing appreciation to tears

for years summer moon

WINTER WHISTLES

Winter Whistles through clear blue skies
filtering out contamination lies
while twigs branches lay naked bare
because of roots being striped of negligence care

Concrete smothers underground soil
preventing nutrients absorption
to sprout suns excellence warmth beauty

The hope of sea defrost station
is crying ice melt down circulation
appreciating the stimulant of season Winter Whistles
knowing life's mission brings no contradiction

UNDERGROUND STEEL

Stirs its wheels through racing reels
passing little towns
with no acknowledgement of frowns
on the clowns greed for power
that's leaving many homeless sour

Another mile and there's rows of corporate suits
brief cases engaging in many pursuits
monopolizing on capitalisms power
cutting throats in its subtle mire

Take a left and note the shopping of wants
as the live band ignites the hustle and bustle
stirring the crowd to carry out life's shuffle
how about we stop for a little cappachino
must start the day on top of the game

The carts and platforms are packed tight
with united nations passing stations
taking passengers to its destinations
Merchants, panhandlers, business deals
luncheons, concerts, love stories, broken hearts
death, life, tragedies, miracles all transpires
down in the gloomy looking chaotic world
yet we don't fret or fear
It's the Underground Steel

EMOTIONAL MIXTURES

UNDERSTANDING

He promises to love you for you
and never take you for granted
He says I want to marry you
and have you bear my children
Oh please he says let me wash your feet
cause baby even they smell sweet

My darling my eyes are focus on you only
I promise you will never have to feel lonely
Just say you'll be mine forever
and you can depend on my support to leave you never

OK you say feeling I have struck gold
you had no idea how fast those words would turn cold
There was a moment he loved you for you
but now he's complaining about everything you do

When you said yes I would be the mother of your children
you had no idea the father was included
You've liked the idea of him washing your feet
but now he's saying that they stink

You can't understand why you feel so lonely
he did say he was focused on you only
But now he has had a change of heart
which is interestingly becoming his art

I must admit I'm a bit confused
I can't understand what he's putting me through
Acknowledgement of the black man's fall
is why I stand by his side so tall

Loving him was all I wanted to do
but now I see the importance of loving me too
What will I do with this commitment
should I confess I need distance

No cause that's an easy way out
and girlfriend you know we have too much clout
We will continue to be who we are
the star who has gotten us thus far

Have faith eventually he'll get it together
it's to his benefit that he leaves you never
And for some strange reason he loses all senses
you can proudly say you did your part
despite consequences
Can we truly now say we have understanding?
Well let's just be thankful
that we're still standing

NEVER LET GO

Your eyes when I gaze into them look

wild, crazy, passionate, filled with love

make me want to go down deep down

where I've never dreamed of going before

And oh how pleasant it is

to feel you at your most vulnerable

it taste too good to good to let go

KNOCK, KNOCK

Knock, Knock

Who's there?

Me the one you've chased down continuously
let me in, I'm ready to show you how its done
remembering your experience has been with none
I should have appreciated the privilege sooner
but something was preventing me

Knock, Knock

I'm sorry no one is home
the invitation grew lonely and wondered away
finally realizing you were not worth the wait

CRAVING

Craving the attention of a man
sometimes unable one to stand
Needing the relief of floating on clouds
yet it seems never to be carried out
Written in the book this craving would exist
not quite realizing it would be this intense
Ready to slam the door in its face
when reopened its spirit still can be traced
What's one to do in this predicament
take comfort in knowing many share your sentiment

WANNA HAVE YOU AROUND

Can you come and chill wit me
I just wanna have you around absorb your energy
see your smile, watch you cap a tude
feel your hug and taste your kiss on my lips
you're so sweet
I just wanna have you around
how about we do breakfast or brunch
then come home and visit the sack for a nap
later on hit the laundry and while its washing
go shopping for food that will later on
put us in the mood

Oh let's not forget the suits from the cleaners
we'll need it during the week when meeting with vendors
I think they see you more than me
and I'm wearing the wedding ring
It's true we're both trying to make it happen
in keeping up with life actions
but we can't forget to maintain us
strengthening our relationship with trust is a must

So come on and chill wit me your wifey
I just wanna have you around

CONFESSION

I want a man to love and I'm not ashamed
to admit it to the world
This necessity of mine is a basic need
it's not out of greed
It's how I was designed
there is no need for me to be criticized

I understand women's independence
but it should not be apart from her man
We need them to successfully stand

Come on sisters confess the need for love from our brothers
We need their touch, kiss, strength
and intensity of their beings
WE NEED THEIR LOVE, so go ahead and
CONFESS, CONFESS, CONFESS, CONFESSION

I want to be treated like a women
not like a lady of the night
which means we have to put up a hard fight
Society says that sex sells it's time we tell them
to burn in hell

A woman is what our brothers want and need
why are we depriving them of this basic need
Come on brothers confess
the need for love from your Sisters

You need her trust, delicacy, understanding
YOU NEED A WOMEN'S LOVE, so go ahead and
CONFESS, CONFESS, CONFESS, CONFESSION

I want to be understood that
I'm not trying to change the world
just share my feeling on it's exploitations

Confession to me is expressing truth
which is why I
CONFESS, CONFESS, CONFESS, CONFESSION

SYSTEM'S GLITCH

Why you playing wit me, can't you see I'm not
in the mood to be fooled

Member when we first met you drooled
so stop trying to act like you weren't whipped
when reflecting back you refused influenced sip

Your reaction was straight up poland spring
ignoring any and all possible distractions
that was trying to encounter some action
dismissing folks like I was the only one that exist
until your trigger got eager to experience new grass
and automatically your name
was changed to Jackass

Don't take me wrong I appreciate our Kings
they're the only ones who can make my heart sang
sweet melodies and cry life's blues
so I would never want to lose their shoes
standing by my side
even if its fabricated in the imaginary mind

loving the option of pointing the stick
narrowing in on the chocolate swirl flava's
even though there's times you want to grace
his shield with brick's favor
you quickly mature not wanting
to deal with the manure
It's better not to mess with the wheels
temporary insanity may just be how he deals

So how bout we take another route
have his back, we know its our heart desire
no need to drag his ego in the mire
we gotta work toward quenching the fire

It's obvious there's a glitch in the system
blinding the sight of wisdom's
connection to family union
get out of the game
its bringing too many of us to shame

SITTING ALONE

Sitting alone wondering why I'm alone

perfect I'm not by any means

skills however inherited from the supreme

getting someone to notice me for me

appreciating me un-hypocritically

does not seem to exist

Get out more, it's when you're least expected

engulf in creativity is what they advise

I continue to do it all and is still sitting alone

wondering why I'm alone

DEEP

May I try you out and see how deep your love can go

I want you to go deep into my soul

making me appreciate home

enjoying the experience of feeling whole

as it melts off loneliness cold

that's trying to force me into a bliss

as it persist for nature's love to be dismissed

Should I accept this

to do so would be a disgrace

Please know I'm not desperate

I just need to know

how deep your love can go

LIKING IT

Liking it, oh yeah, I'm sure you are

this flava chocolate is the best by far

Soft and cushiony is its center

which keeps one warm especially winter

Saturated with fragrant oils seeped deep into its wells

having the power to intoxicate one's soul

making it pleasant to dwell

The hands are racing to feel and touch

knowing the gain will be much

Liking it? Oh yeah you are

this chocolate flava is the best by far

COMMITMENT

You ask me on the first night if I want to commit

knowing you're so very far from the submit

you talk about not playing games

yet you're the ring leader with no shame

in the long run you want me to become bitter

but my soul couldn't be sweeter

FALL

Fall is here but I'm feeling extremely hot

I'm talking melting chocolate hot

you know when it's dripping down the middle

landing right in the center needing assistance to enter

absorbing music melodies sighs of relief from life's grief

reassuring soul survival it gives thanks

for it's pleasurable arrival

Oh how relaxing that would be

especially in the fall

ESCAPE

Escape into my walls that lead to the halls

of fragrance vulnerability intoxications exfoliations

threw stimulations gift of sense

It's natural spiritual and sensual durable

caressing miracles gold mine

which can't be sold even upon turning old

it's sacred place is an unforgettable

valuable escape

LOVE AFFAIR

Have you ever had a love affair
with his voice mail service, I have may be
my connection to his service
was my only way to reach him
the only way he would
listen to my heart
the only way he would
not ignore me, so I thought

Hey, everyone listens to their voice mail
you pay for its service
Did I care if his ego blew up, nope!
If he listened and had a good heart
he would hear what my soul was panting
his soul, trust, love
Would he give it…I don't know
Has he given it…I can't say
Do I hope he will surrender one day?

Only and I mean only if his soul craves
to be with mine permanently
It is then I will humbly give him a love
he's been born to inherit, because if not
the love affair was a growing experience
to teach me loving a voice mail service
is no real love affair!

Poetic Diary

JUST BEING HUMAN

WORK PLACE

Dealing with people is sometimes an unwanted job
A task we must take on despite the size of the mob

A sense of humor is what we all need
cause we're dealing with different levels of greed

Lots of humility oh yeah that's good
cause it helps pay for our neighborhood

Don't by into the false affection
the outcome is unlimited negative deflection

They'll hate you today and love you tomorrow
let that not be the cause of your sorrow

We must learn to take things in stride
never letting go of our pride

Yes dealing with people is sometimes an unwanted job
But let's never forget we too are a part of that mob

FACELESS LOVE

Faceless love is awaiting at the door
with one knee on the floor
desperately wanting to be let in
if not will knock it down cursing frowns
of frustrations for simplicity not adding up
with life's mixtures ingredients of love
kindness, humility, intelligence
ambition, sultry and peace
why the grief

Open the door and show your face to love
before it's too late to enjoy dates
ice-cream cones with sprinkles
skips in the park after dark
and little offspring joyous ring

Are you willing to let it all fall in abyss never to be missed
none of this is making sense it's pretense faceless love

never should one settle into playing the game
it brings shame to the authenticity of love
open the door and reveal your face

THE SCHEME

Butt kissers, yes masters, crack lickers, men pleasers
selling souls for fabricated schemes
that has nothing to do with your dreams

How you think Hitler ruled
don't be fooled in massaging their sass
your grass will wither and filter
out its gold to the cold

Why don't you just be bold and grown
get a backbone hold your own
for truth's sake

No need to pretend that fake is real
we know the deal
patting backs while filling your sacks
not realizing your so called nobility
is losing it's equity due to testosterone fire

Where's the extinguisher to support its hire
in unwanted dire situations powerless realization
being locked away in a bolted safe
ignoring the danger of life benefit sake

What a disgrace of work ethics moral
it's time we all came around
and said NO
having confidence their scheme will blow

DRIFT

As we drift through our beings
to find meaning of our purpose
hips must be firmly in place
to secure talents space
sifting through all joints
so as to anoint one's art from the heart

While pleasing for its gain
from rains pain as it leaves stains
searching for sanity through life's vanity
for its clear reflection of mirror peace

As we drift folks in lost of their art
ignorantly and intentionally shooting darts
to dispose of our jewels

Don't runaway despite folks dismay
in their own burglarious situation
as they mock humility and disgrace modesty
refusing to appreciate one's gift
and acknowledge talents graced from above
We must continue to show love
through life's Art as we Drift

OVERLOAD

I woke up in the early morning
being thankful for the nights rest
yet inside my head I'm still a mess
where did my rejuvenation run
it certainly left me behind

I'm on overload, not sure where to go
trying to get things straight
yet there's a big black hole sucking me toward its way

Feeling the water trickling down my skin
allows its doors to vent sin as I scrub away at its toxics
watching it spiral down the drainage
brings little satisfaction
Can't hide from daily duties got to keep moving forward
hoping back stabbing knives will be kind
considering our predicament is intertwined

Can't it find its self esteem?
and stop chasing down power insecurities greed
that contradict nature's evidence
Analyze it, where is the sense

I'm on overload, not sure where to go
trying to get things straight yet there's a big black hole
sucking me toward its way

LUST PAIN/HAIKU

Rain unwanted pain
innocent embryo pays
for lust pleasure gain

TORNADO

A Tornado spirals out of control
viciously trying to rip out my soul
Determined to hang on for dear life
striving not to give up in the fight
Realizing my faith is at stake
pleading desperately for it not to break

CONCRETE RAIN

Pit Pat, Pit pat

Waterfalls absorbs on skin leaf back
dripping rain drops on head and neck
rolling of shoulders in knack sack life stress
depleting nutrients needed full deck

Pit Pat, Pit pat

Drizzle midst downpour seeps into nerves swerves
discouraging ambition drive to update stride
ignore its lack of pride

Instead

Kick off shoes and socks
its time to wring dry, angry cries
bake pies to sweeten veins
guaranteed to minimize pain

Pit Pat, Pit pat

Soak soul in hot tub oils
letting chastity runneth over
dripping into cracks wooden peaks
it speaks to neighbors ears
injecting contagious joyous tears
in victory of conquering concrete rain

TECHNOLOGY OBSESSIONS

Technology has made its way into the human race
though has claimed to be our best friend
can't be traced when tears are shed and shoulders need drying
it's obsessions is beneath fellow feelings
it's objective is to detect your dealings

Have you noticed the convenience of cell phones
lap tops and note pads superficial promise of confidentiality
it's your best friend technology reality
to snatch away privacy power control for worship
I'm the god you serve it brags
even if you feel it's undeserved

Take note of your leisure time spent on the couch
while you and your partner
scream and shout intimacies pleasures
Is there anyone watching from DTV
if so I think it's obscene that you pay them to watch you
mmmh…
tell me who's being screwed by Technology Obsessions

SELF ABSORPTION

Is poisonous, it does nothing but take
embellishing a smile that's absolutely fake

Being in denial of its action ignoring the fractions
of its inflicted self satisfaction
for absence manipulated excuses

Will comfort when its benefit is in sight
but don't take too long to give
the standing ovation for appreciation
cause it will surely take to flight

Failing to reminisce on sincere gift giving
it's only expected and deserved in its life living

Self absorption will try to suck you dry but don't let it
move on to the next until you conquer the conquest

EXPERIMENTATION'S DECEIT

Experiments leave many in questionable predicaments
not always for benefit circumstance
quarreling common sense rejection of dark dense
that prevents strength growth to
influence nature's flow of true beauty

Its undercover whispering sounds searches for innocence vulnerability
to humiliate pride's stake
with a grin embellishing sin's vindication of degradation
what a pitiful situation of outcome experimentation

If acknowledgment is in truth space
it will bow down to mercies grace revealing face
for repentance actions of purification
rejecting contamination subtle stimulations
to corrupt the soul dignity's grace

If ignored of its power your being will become sour
groping for the next hit leaving you powerless to quit
its manipulation foul addiction of enemy's chain
destroying the gift of life to flourish

Experimentation deceit if not cautious
will cause your defeat

LOVE'S FREEZE

Why must true love feel burdensome
jeopardizing freedom dance
can we prance the ultimate experience
with sighs from grief's relief
that makes our wrongs strong for its sincere acceptance

Though we must fight to stand for soul truth
it's journey sometimes makes our heart blue
while riding the race of love's consumption
overjoyed however of being rescued from its death
tightly holding on to its tender righteousness

I cuddle nature's intuition as I bow down
submitting to its beauty
and accepting humility knees fall
while it melts love's freeze

Poetic Diary

HEALTHY REFLECTIONS

LOVE, LOVE, LOVE

A little if you may
It's simple

Thank you, please, excuse me
and mean it

Cry, smile, laugh
and feel it

Apologize, forgive, listen
and want to

Share, care, hug
and yearn to

Sincerely
Tenderly
Un hypocritically

Love, Love, Love

TO LIVE

To live is to let live

To let live is to not be judgmental

To not be judgmental is know your own demons

To know your own demons is to accept the truth

To accept the truth is to feel pain

To feel pain is to shed tears

To shed tears is to grow

To grow is to mature

Maturity enables us to love

And love allows us to live

TO BE IN FEAR AGAIN

To be in fear again I would not want to be
never once did I feel free
free to speak, dance, laugh, or cry
my emotions were locked up inside

Oh I was taught right from wrong
being governed with fear did what made me strong
fear to do wrong has been a part of my life
for so long which is why I must release this song

Oppose wrong don't fear it or you will become it's slave
its strength will prevent you from making valuable trades
one trade is to love which throws fear outside
brightening up your soul enabling you to shine

To be in fear again I would not want to be
I love being set free

HOLY WAR

Stop and listen to your soul as it speaks
something is going on something is going on I tell you
It's the preparation for the holy war
that will save our souls for a perfect tomorrow

A good heart mixture is the needed ingredient
and only the originator of love can detect it
so listen to the architect of your design
and never disappear from his side

Cultivate love in your dealings whole soul
never forgetting where it is bestowed

Yes the holy war will take place
and the originator of love is the only one
who can secure your space

Keep your heart open and receptive to his call
because something is going on
something is going on I tell you

DID YOU BRING ME HERE...

Did you bring me here just to let me walk away
I can't go back to the way it was
stifling cold and loneliness filtrated my soul

When I walked away there was a sense of relief
but in my heart I felt grief
years I tried to build relationships based on truth and trust
when I made a decision to preserve my inner happiness
so called friends disappeared like particles of dust

It confirmed life's valuable lesson
trust your intuition and be truthful to yourself
because when all else fails
it is this that will allow you to sail

As you travel through life's trail
tap into your soul and seek for its gold
allowing peace to permeate your being

As you experience blindness seeing your mind
on loose chains groping for stabilities connection
to help you get through this world's rejection

I know you did not bring me here
just to let me walk away
I'm going forward it's the only way!

MANIPULATION

Manipulation smiles in your face

steals your trust without a trace

skilled in how it plays the game

never once feeling shamed

If allowed will control your life

as long as their benefit is in site

who's to blame for this manipulation

the who did not exercise stipulation

BARE

Bare your soul
until it's cold
then it's sold

Bare your heart
is when you start
to reveal your art

Bare your self
and income your wealth

ELEVATION

Elevation is where our minds deserve to be

looking down on nature's beauty

The love joy and laughter it sings

caresses the heart giving permission

to embellish one's art

Introducing the mind to elevation

shaking off contaminations and fraudulence

of enemy scheme to depress dreams

Don't throw away keys to the mind giving into slavery sin

Ignore their efforts unlock your mind and breath…

while climbing the mountain to deserved elevation

STILL

Still is hard if you will

we must accept it still

Sit, Stand, run, or walk

appreciation for still is life's will

Upon accepting life's will

there's enjoyment in being still

FREEDOM EXPLOITATIONS

To be free we reveal what's sacred

feeling that it will bring liberation

As time goes by we sink into degradation

enveloping some of us into

unwanted situations and isolation

oh how we've been fully manipulated

by freedom exploitations

TAKE CONTROL

Reject the cold, nurture your soul

who wants to be left alone upon turning old

Open your heart even when it hurts

it will get you pass life's curse

Accept love, support and honor

don't allow your being to grow sour

Take control!

RESTORE MY FAITH

Restore my faith in the human race

it's their help I need to keep my face

No matter how they behave

I must remember deep in their souls

they have the potential to show love

MIND YOUR MIND

Mind your mind

and help it find its way to freedom

dine its hunger with vitaminization

to help it maintain immunization

against ignorance action to strip one's pride

until there's no where to hide accept its bondage

please take time to mind your mind

as it finds its way to freedom

APPRECIATE SELF

To be alone with yourself
is to appreciate your divine design
See it as it truthfully is made in the image of the most high

Know we have the desire to flourish
even if it has not been previously nourished

Spend time and listen to yourself
it will communicate your purpose assisting you
in staying alienated from this world's circus

Please hear me out on this and understand
I'm not trying to Dis
yourself is a part of the grand plan
without appreciating yourself, how will you stand?

KEEPING IT REAL

Keeping it real, means keeping it true
it means being honest, it means being righteous
it means honoring justice
So if you ain't gonna try and be that
hold off in saying keeping it real

Because it means being true to your soul
which won't be compromised when offered gold
it means being honest in your dealings
when translated there will be no stealing
it means loving righteousness sweet tenderness
while not mistaken it for your neighbors weakness
it means demonstrating justice when dealing with others
not just when your circumstances come uncovered

So if you ain't gonna try and be that
hold off in saying keeping it real
cause you making the atmosphere ill
with too many drills infecting negative thrills
so how bout if you chill in saying keeping it real
until we see the value of being real

THE PLAYER

The real player is no hater it climbs the latter to success

never letting obstacles allow for its rest

understanding the psyche is at its best

when seeking ways to multiply gain in the game

Accepting the reality of freedom's warranty

keeping distance from household drug mentalities

realizing benefits will ascend high

ignoring lies while dodging falls

the player stands tall amidst it all

confident rules remain the same

contemplating mind never be put to shame

for talents claim to score on the board

earning life's sweet success

THE BRIDGE

Did you forget I would be there always
proved it
sealed it
protected it for you

Why? because I love you
created you
embraced you

You're going through bad times
should I drop you
dismiss you
let you go
cut you off

Listen to your intuition
because it will set off your ignition
of my love for you

I'd already proved it
sealed it
protected it

Because I created you
embraced you
and will forever accept you

Never let anyone tell you
I've dismissed you
let you go
cut you off

Acknowledge the truth
that will set you free
and maintain the bridge
that will save your life

ACCEPTANCE/HAIKU

Accept love grace please

release its energy free

from enemy chains

Dedicated To P.S.190

BE YOU

Congratulations to the graduating class
who made it through life's most vulnerable stages
and is still standing tall, I tip my hat off to you all
It's obvious you've endured your falls
I want you to tap yourself on the back
and remember through life journey
to continuously do just that

From what I hear rumor has it
you're heading to Junior High
I know you're excited, mixed with fear
but from personal experience I know you will Persevere
Open those books along with your mind
and I guarantee that you will fly
through life's discrimination
because wisdom books will give you
the determination

Your life will be transformed into pearls
allowing your soul to swirl in any world you choose
just make sure it feels sincerely free
making your destiny happy

Alright, so at times it will be difficult
but I beg you to continue to push on with your pursuits
get involved even if you feel like a bump on a log
remember a log can bring warmth's fire
and that's what you've ignited in the hearts desire
of your parents, teachers and community this day

So once again, I say to the graduating
class stand tall and pat yourself on the back
because sweet hearts you all deserve just that

Thank you for the privilege and
Remember to be you!

ASPIRATIONS FOR LIFE

- Always love yourself first, the creator designed you that way.
- If you have to chase, go ahead, just never loose your dignity.
- Friends are forever, even if you hit their last nerve.
- Never let anyone control your mind......it's slavery.
- Family is forever, even if it's dysfunctional.
- Smile, even if ya don't want to, it's good for the soul.
- Love everyone unconditionally, just not their habits.
- Never be self righteous, it conditions you to hate yourself unknowingly.
- Appreciate the things in life that's free, it sweetens your soul.
- Never forget the promise from above, it will continue to enable you to love.

PERSONAL JOURNAL

HEAL YOUR HEART

_____

_____

_____

_____

_____

_____

_____

_____

_____

_____

_____

_____

_____

_____

HEAL YOUR HEART

HEAL YOUR HEART

HEAL YOUR HEART

HEAL YOUR HEART

_____

_____

_____

_____

_____

_____

_____

_____

_____

_____

_____

_____

_____

_____

_____

_____

HEAL YOUR HEART

HEAL YOUR HEART

HEAL YOUR HEART

_____

_____

_____

_____

_____

_____

_____

_____

_____

_____

_____

_____

_____

_____

_____

_____

HEAL YOUR HEART

_____

_____

_____

_____

_____

_____

_____

_____

_____

_____

_____

_____

_____

_____

_____

HEAL YOUR HEART

_____

_____

_____

_____

_____

_____

_____

_____

_____

_____

_____

_____

_____

_____

_____

_____

HEAL YOUR HEART

HEAL YOUR HEART

HEAL YOUR HEART

Poetic Diary

HEAL YOUR HEART

HEAL YOUR HEART

HEAL YOUR HEART

HEAL YOUR HEART

Poetic Diary

HEAL YOUR HEART

Poetic Diary

HEAL YOUR HEART

_____

_____

_____

_____

_____

_____

_____

_____

_____

_____

_____

_____

_____

_____

_____

_____

Poetic Diary

HEAL YOUR HEART

_____

_____

_____

_____

_____

_____

_____

_____

_____

_____

_____

_____

_____

_____

HEAL YOUR HEART

HEAL YOUR HEART

_____

_____

_____

_____

_____

_____

_____

_____

_____

_____

_____

_____

_____

_____

HEAL YOUR HEART

HEAL YOUR HEART

_____

_____

_____

_____

_____

_____

_____

_____

_____

_____

_____

_____

_____

_____

HEAL YOUR HEART

_____

_____

_____

_____

_____

_____

_____

_____

_____

_____

_____

_____

_____

_____

HEAL YOUR HEART

_____

_____

_____

_____

_____

_____

_____

_____

_____

_____

_____

_____

_____

_____

_____

_____

Poetic Diary

HEAL YOUR HEART

Poetic Diary

HEAL YOUR HEART

HEAL YOUR HEART

_____

_____

_____

_____

_____

_____

_____

_____

_____

_____

_____

_____

_____

_____

HEAL YOUR HEART

_____

_____

_____

_____

_____

_____

_____

_____

_____

_____

_____

_____

_____

_____

_____

_____

HEAL YOUR HEART

HEAL YOUR HEART

_____

_____

_____

_____

_____

_____

_____

_____

_____

_____

_____

_____

_____

_____

_____

_____

HEAL YOUR HEART

HEAL YOUR HEART

HEAL YOUR HEART

_____

_____

_____

_____

_____

_____

_____

_____

_____

_____

_____

_____

_____

Poetic Diary

HEAL YOUR HEART

_____

_____

_____

_____

_____

_____

_____

_____

_____

_____

_____

_____

_____

_____

_____

_____

_____

HEAL YOUR HEART

Poetic Diary

HEAL YOUR HEART

_____

_____

_____

_____

_____

_____

_____

_____

_____

_____

_____

_____

_____

_____

_____

_____

HEAL YOUR HEART

_____

_____

_____

_____

_____

_____

_____

_____

_____

_____

_____

_____

_____

_____

_____

HEAL YOUR HEART

Poetic Diary

HEAL YOUR HEART

_____

_____

_____

_____

_____

_____

_____

_____

_____

_____

_____

_____

_____

_____

_____

_____

_____

Poetic Diary

HEAL YOUR HEART

_____

_____

_____

_____

_____

_____

_____

_____

_____

_____

_____

_____

_____

_____

_____

HEAL YOUR HEART

_____

_____

_____

_____

_____

_____

_____

_____

_____

_____

_____

_____

_____

_____

_____

_____

_____

_____

Poetic Diary

HEAL YOUR HEART

_____

_____

_____

_____

_____

_____

_____

_____

_____

_____

_____

_____

_____

_____

_____

HEAL YOUR HEART

_____

_____

_____

_____

_____

_____

_____

_____

_____

_____

_____

_____

_____

_____

HEAL YOUR HEART

_____

_____

_____

_____

_____

_____

_____

_____

_____

_____

_____

_____

_____

_____

HEAL YOUR HEART

_____

_____

_____

_____

_____

_____

_____

_____

_____

_____

_____

_____

_____

_____

_____

_____

_____

HEAL YOUR HEART

_____

_____

_____

_____

_____

_____

_____

_____

_____

_____

_____

_____

_____

_____

Poetic Diary

HEAL YOUR HEART

HEAL YOUR HEART

Poetic Diary

AUTOBIOGRAPHY

Tracey Howard is a native New Yorker who was born in the heart of the South Bronx. It is there where she experienced the value of strength in the midst of insecurity. It is there where her imagination created people who made her feel like a star, despite her imperfections and quirks. The inspiration given to her was to be a star in your own world and once that realization was in place, she was able to embark on an adventure that lead to the experimentation of life on the West Coast. The hospitality of the Pacific Ocean mesmerized her being with deeper meaning of human nature's flow bringing her a mellow glow. Her journey did not stop there it craved for the Hispanic flare of the Dominicana flava that graced her with many favors. The deep rich dark soil brought her spirit to an exciting boil that simmered into contentment leaving an aroma of soft mint. As she continues to coast through life her observations, meditations, stipulations, manipulations, inspirations, vindications and realizations is helping her maintain a life of peace power and self worth.

Giving back to the community has always been one of her priorities. Through her life journey she has volunteered with numerous organizations actively participating in workshops and progressive personal assistant programs.

She enjoys reading, writing, traveling, walks through parks and quality time spent with family and friends.

Please feel free to express your thoughts and comments in regards to Poetic Diary by sending an email to Poeticdiary2003@yahoo.com

www.ingramcontent.com/pod-product-compliance
Lightning Source LLC
Chambersburg PA
CBHW030315290526
45785CB00001B/369